The P
of the
Blessed Virgin Mary
by
St Bonaventure

St Athanasius Press
All Rights Reserved 2016

ISBN-13: 978-1533301048

ISBN-10: 1533301042

St Athanasius Press
2016

Specializing in Reprinting Catholic Classics!

CONTENTS

AUTHOR'S PREFACE

"Take hold on her, and she shall exalt thee: thou shalt be glorified by her, when thou shalt embrace her. She shall give to thy head increase of graces, and protect thee with a noble crown." (Prov. 4:8-9.)

Glory be to God on high, and thanksgiving, and the voice of praise, who at one time by the mysteries of prophecy, at another by oracles from Heaven, again by the reading of the Gospel, and now by the mouth of preachers, in many ways and by divers channels, most sincerely urges and invites us to honor the Virgin Mary, the Queen of Heaven and of the Angels; that by her holy merits, most worthy of all acceptance, we, being delivered from the depths of hell, may be inscribed by her in the ranks of the angels. Wherefore, although Solomon spoke the aforesaid words of Wisdom, nevertheless the Holy Spirit, by a mystical application, intends them to be understood of the most excellent Virgin Mary.

By means of these words, dearly beloved, He is drawing you to His love, and by various promises is attracting and softening your hearts, that you may enjoy His divine embraces. His meaning is that you will obtain four wonderful gifts, if this glorious Virgin is joined to you by a spiritual bond, and is embraced by you in the arms of fervent desire, with great reverence and devotion. First, she will bring you exaltation; and she shall exalt thee; secondly, glorification; and thou shalt be glorified by her; thirdly, the abundance of graces; she shall give to thy head increase of graces; fourthly, the unfading crown of perpetual glory, and protect thee with a noble crown. Therefore I beseech thee, dearly beloved and most desired, do not repel so noble and so beautiful a virgin; do not make little of so admirable and revered a queen as the Virgin Mary: lest, if she should see herself despised by you, you will be, I will not say, deprived of such great favors, but, which God forbid, you will incur perpetual evils. Expand the bosom of your mind to serve her, prepare your heart to praise and glorify her, lose your tongue, and with swift service hasten to please her. For there is no doubt that from her nearness to you, you will become more devout, from contact with her you will grow more pure, from her embrace you will abound more in grace and be more resplendent in purity. That I may give you an occasion of obtaining such great gifts, I send you the Psalter of this most Holy Virgin, put together and composed indeed by my feeble intelligence, but with her grace and help; by means of it you will praise with divers hymns, now her virginity and chastity, now her fecundity and sanctity, now her clemency and bounty. You will be able to salute her as full of all grace, or as filled with all knowledge, or as illumined by all understanding and wisdom. There you will bless the Fruit of her glorious womb, the members of His holy body, and the prerogatives of His soul, bestowing all sanctity. There you will invoke the aid of all the choirs of angels to praise her, and of all the multitudes of holy men, the isles of the nations, the heavens, the beauty of all luminaries and of the whole world. There you will beseech her to destroy the power of your spiritual enemies, to obtain for you pardon of all your sins, that she may render the great Judge propitious to you, that she may illumine your deathbed by her gracious presence, and obtain for you joy without end. Therefore, O dearly beloved souls, graciously receive this little gift which I offer you, and strive to draw fruit there from; by means of it frequently praise the Mother of God; and thus perchance she will turn to you her gracious countenance, receiving you to her love, refreshing your soul in the present, and placing upon your head a crown of precious stones in the world to come.

THE PSALTER OF THE BLESSED VIRGIN MARY

PSALM 1

Blessed is the man, O Virgin Mary, who loves thy name; thy grace will comfort his soul.

He will be refreshed as by fountains of water; thou wilt produce in him the fruit of justice.

Blessed art thou among women; by the faith of thy holy heart.

By the beauty of thy body thou surpassest all women; by the excellence of thy sanctity thou surpassest all angels and archangels.

Thy mercy and thy grace are preached everywhere; God has blessed the works of thy hands.

Glory be to the Father, etc.

PSALM 2

Why have our enemies raged and our adversaries devised vain things?

May thy right hand protect us, O Mother of God: as a line of battle terrible in aspect, confounding and destroying them.

Come ye to her, all who labor and are in trouble: and she will give refreshment to your souls.

Draw nigh to her in your temptations: and the serenity of her countenance will bring you peace and confidence.

Bless her with your whole heart: for the earth is full of her mercy.

Glory be to the Father, etc.

PSALM 3

O Lady, why are they multiplied who afflict me? By thy might thou shalt follow them and scatter them.

Loose the bands of our impiety: take away the burden of our sins. Have mercy on me, O Lady, and heal my sickness: take away the grief and anguish of my heart.

Deliver me not into the hands of my enemies: and in the day of my death strengthen thou my soul.

Lead me into the harbor of salvation: and give up for me my spirit to my Maker and Creator.

Glory be to the Father, etc.

PSALM 4

When I called upon thee, thou didst hear me, O Lady: and from thy throne on high thou hast deigned to be mindful of me.

From the roaring of the wild beasts prepared to devour me: and from the hands of them that sought me, thy grace will deliver me.

For thy mercy is kind and thy heart loving: towards all who invoke thy holy name.

Blessed art thou, O Lady, forever: and thy majesty for evermore.

Glorify her, all ye nations in your strength: and all ye peoples of the earth, extol her magnificence.

Glory be to the Father, etc.

PSALM 5

Incline thine ear, O Lady, to hear my prayers: and turn not away from me the beauty of thy face.

Turn our mourning into rejoicing: and our tribulation into joy. May our enemies fall down at our feet: by thy power may their heads be crushed.

Let every tongue praise thee: and let all flesh bless thy holy name.

For thy spirit is sweet above honey: and thy inheritance above the honey and the honeycomb.

Glory be to the Father, etc.

PSALM 6

Lady, let me not be corrected in the wrath of God: nor be judged by Him in His anger.

For the honor of thy name, O Lady: may the Fruit of thy glorious womb be propitious to us.

From the gate of hell and from the depths of the abyss: by thy holy prayers deliver us.

May the eternal gates be opened unto us: that we may declare forever thy wondrous works.

For it is not the dead, nor those in hell, who will praise thee, O Lady: but those who by thy grace will obtain eternal life.

Glory be to the Father etc.

PSALM 7

O my Lady, in thee have I hoped: from my enemies deliver me.

Shut thou the mouth of the lion and his teeth: restrain the lips of those that persecute me.

For thy name's sake delay not to accomplish thy mercy in us.

May the brightness of thy countenance shine upon us: that the Most High may keep remembrance of us.

If the enemy should persecute my soul, O Lady, may I be strengthened by thy help: lest his sword should strike me.

Glory be to the Father, etc.

PSALM 8

O Lady, Our Lord has become our brother and our Savior.

Like the flame in the burning bush, and the dew in the fleece: the Word of God descends into thee forever.

The Holy Spirit hath made thee fruitful: the power of the Most High hath overshadowed thee.

Blessed be thy most pure conception: blessed be thy virginal bringing forth.

Blessed be the purity of thy body: blessed be the sweetness of the mercy of thy heart.

Glory be to the Father, etc.

PSALM 9

I will praise thee, O Lady, with my whole heart: and I will declare among the nations thy praise and glory.

For to thee is due glory, and thanksgiving, and the voice of praise.

May sinners find grace with God by thee, the finder of grace and salvation.

May the humble penitents hope for pardon: heal thou the bruises of their hearts.

In the beauty of peace and wealth rest: thou shalt feed us after the toil of our pilgrimage.

Glory be to the Father, etc.

PSALM 10

I trust in our Lady; because of the sweetness of the mercy of her name.

Her eyes look upon the poor: and her hands are stretched out to the orphan and the widow.

Seek after her from your youth: she will glorify you before the face of the peoples.

Her mercy will deliver us from the multitude of our sins: and will bestow on us fruitfulness of merits.

Stretch out to us thy arm, O glorious Virgin: and do not turn away from us thy glorious face.

Glory be to the Father, etc.

PSALM 11

Save me, O Mother of fair love: fount of clemency and sweetness of piety.

Thou alone makest the circuit of the earth: that thou mayst help those that call upon thee.

Beautiful are thy ways: and thy paths are peaceful.

In thee shine forth the beauty of chastity, the light of justice, and the splendor of truth.

Thou art clothed with the sunrays as with a vesture: resplendent with a shining twelve-starred crown.

Glory be to the Father, etc.

PSALM 12

How long, O Lady, wilt thou forget me and not deliver me in the day of tribulation?

How long will my enemy be exalted above me? By the might of thy strength do thou crush him.

Open the eyes of thy mercy: lest our enemy prevail against us.

We magnify thee, the finder of grace, by whom the ages of the world are restored.

Thou art exalted above the choirs of angels: pray for us before the throne of God.

Glory be to the Father, etc.

PSALM 13

Our foolish enemy hath said in his heart: I will follow after and take him, and my hand shall slay him.

Arise, O Lady, and prevent him, and supplant him: destroy all his machinations.

Thy beauty astonishes the sun and the moon; the angelic powers serve and obey thee.

By thy gentle touch the sick are healed: by thy rose-sweet fragrance the dead revive.

Virgin Mother of God, He whom the whole world cannot contain was enclosed within thee, being made Man.

Glory be to the Father, etc.

PSALM 14

O Lady, who shall dwell in the tabernacle of God? Or who shall rest with the leaders of the people?

The poor in spirit, and the pure of heart, the meek, the peaceful, and the mourners.

Be mindful, O Lady, that thou speak for us good things: and that thou mayest turn away the indignation of thy Son from us.

O sinners, let us embrace the footprints of Mary, and cast ourselves at her blessed feet.

Let us hold her fast, nor let her go: until we deserve to be blessed by her.

Glory be to the Father, etc.

PSALM 15

Preserve me, O Lady, for I have hoped in thee: do thou bestow on me the dew of thy grace.

Thy virginal womb has begotten the Son of the Most High.

Blessed be thy breasts, by which thou hast nourished the Savior with deific milk.

Let us give praise to the glorious Virgin: whosoever ye be that have found grace and mercy through her.

Give glory to her name: and praise forever her conception and her birth.

Glory be to the Father, etc.

PSALM 16

Hear, O Lady, my justice and my love: remove from me my tribulations.

I will give praise to thee in the voice of rejoicing: when thou shalt magnify thy mercy in me.

Imitate her, ye holy virgins of God: as Agnes, Barbara, Dorothy, and Catherine have done.

Give honor to her by the voice of your lips: thus have Agatha, Lucy, Margaret, and Cecilia received her grace.

She will give you as your Spouse the Son of the Father: and a crown incomparably radiant with the lilies of Paradise.

Glory be to the Father, etc.

PSALM 17

I will love thee, O Lady of heaven and earth: and I will call upon thy name in the nations.

Give praise to her, ye who are troubled in heart: and she will strengthen you against your enemies.

Give to us, O Lady, the grace of thy breasts: from the dropping milk of thy sweetness refresh the inmost souls of thy children.

Honor her, O all ye religious: for she is your helper and your special advocate.

Be thou our refreshment, glorious Mother of Christ: for thou art the admirable foundation of the religious life.

Glory be to the Father, etc.

PSALM 18

The heavens declare thy glory: and the fragrance of thine unguents is spread abroad among the nations.

Sigh ye unto her, ye lost sinners: and she will lead you to the harbor of pardon.

In hymns and canticles knock at her heart: and she will rain down upon you the grace of her sweetness.

Glorify her, ye just, before the throne of God: for by the fruit of her womb you have worked justice.

Praise ye her, ye heaven of heavens: and the whole earth will glorify her name.

Glory be to the Father, etc.

PSALM 19

Thou shalt hear us, O Lady, in the day of tribulation: and by our prayers turn to us thy merciful countenance.

Cast us not off in the time of our death: but help the soul, when it shall have left the body.

Send an angel to meet it: by whom it may be defended from the enemy.

Show unto it the most serene Judge of ages: who for thy grace will bestow pardon.

Let it feel thy refreshment in its torments: and grant to it a place among the elect of God.

Glory be to the Father, etc.

PSALM 20

O Lady, in thy strength our heart shall rejoice: and in the sweetness of thy name our soul shall be consoled.

From thy throne send us wisdom: by which we shall be sweetly enlightened in all truth.

Give us grace to abstain from carnal desires: that the light of thy grace may arise in our hearts.

How sweet are thy words, O Lady, to them that love thee: how sweet is the shower of thy graces.

I will sing unto thy glory and honor: and in thy name I will glory forever.

Glory be to the Father, etc.

PSALM 21

O God, my God: let Him look at thy merits in me, ever Virgin Mary.

O my Lady, I have cried to thee by day and by night: and thou hast done mercy with thy servant.

Because I have hoped in thy mercy: thou hast taken away from me everlasting reproach.

Mine enemies have mocked me on every side: but thou under the shadow of thy hand hast bestowed good refreshment on me.

Let all the families of the peoples adore thee: and let all the orders of the angels glorify thee.

Glory be to the Father, etc.

PSALM 22

The Lord rules me, O Virgin Mother of God: because thou hast turned on me thy gracious countenance.

Blessed are thy most resplendent eyes: which thou deignest to turn on sinners.

Blessed is the light and the splendor of thy countenance: blessed is the grace of thy face.

Blessed be the mercy of thy hands: blessed be the stream of thy virginal milk.

Let the prophets and apostles of God bless thee: let martyrs, confessors, and virgins sing praise to thee.

Glory be to the Father, etc.

PSALM 23

The earth is the Lord's and the fullness thereof: but thou, O most holy Mother, reignest with Him forever.

Thou art clothed with glory and beauty: every precious stone is thy covering and thy clothing.

The brightness of the sun is upon thy head: the beauty of the moon is beneath thy feet.

Shining orbs adorn thy throne: the morning stars glorify thee forever.

Be mindful of us, O Lady, in thy good pleasure: and make us worthy to glorify thy name.

Glory be to the Father, etc.

PSALM 24

To thee, O Lady, have I lifted up my soul: in the judgment of God, by the help of thy prayers, I shall not be ashamed.

Let not my adversaries make game of me: for those who trust in thee are strengthened.

Let not the snares of death prevail against me: and the camps of the malignant not hinder my steps.

Crush their violence in thy might: and with mildness meet my soul.

Be my guide unto my fatherland: and deign to join me to thy angelic hosts.

Glory be to the Father, etc.

PSALM 25

Judge me, O Lady, for I have departed from my innocence: but because I have hoped in thee I shall not become weak.

Enkindle my heart with the fire of thy love: and with the girdle of chastity bind my reins.

For thy mercy and thy clemency are before my eyes: and I was delighted in the voice of thy praise.

O Lady, I have loved the beauty of thy face: and I have revered thy sacred majesty.

Praise ye her name, for she is holy: let her wonders be declared forever.

Glory be to the Father, etc.

PSALM 26

O Lady, may thy light be the splendor of my countenance: and let the serenity of thy grace shine upon my mind.

Raise up my head: and I will sing a psalm to thy name.

Turn not away thy face from me: for from my youth up I have greatly desired thy beauty and thy grace.

I have loved thee and sought after thee, O Queen of Heaven: withdraw not thy mercy and thy grace from thy servant.

I will give praise to thee in the nations: and I will honor the throne of thy glory.

Glory be to the Father, etc.

PSALM 27

To thee, O Lady, will I cry, and thou shalt hear me: in the voice of thy praise thou wilt make me glad.

Have mercy on me in the day of my trouble: and in the light of thy truth deliver me.

Blessed be thou, O Lady: to the uttermost ends of the earth.

The sanctuary which thy hands have established: is the holy temple of thy body.

Thy conscience is pure and undefiled: a place of propitiation and the holy dwelling of God.

Glory be to the Father, etc.

PSALM 28

Bring to Our Lady, O ye sons of God: bring to Our Lady praise and reverence.

Give strength to thy saints, O holy Mother: and thy blessing to those who praise and glorify thee.

Hear the groans of those who sigh to thee: and despise not the prayers of those who invoke thy name.

Let thy hand be ready to help me: and thy ear inclined to my prayer.

Let the heavens and the earth bless thee: the sea and the world.

Glory be to the Father, etc.

PSALM 29

I will exalt thee, O Lady, for thou hast taken me up: thou wilt deliver me from the wicked enemy.

Turn to me and quicken me, from the gates of death lead me back: and from the rivers of tribulation which have surrounded me.

For the sake of thy empire and the magnificence of thy right hand: break and scatter all my enemies.

And I will offer thee a sacrifice of praise: and I will most devoutly exalt thy glory.

Rejoice, ye Heavens, and be glad, O Earth: because Mary will console her servants and will have mercy on her poor.

Glory be to the Father, etc.

PSALM 30

In thee, O Lady, have I hoped, let me never be confounded: receive me in thy grace.

Thou art my strength and my refuge: my consolation and my protection.

To thee, O Lady, have I cried, when my heart was in anguish: and thou hast heard me from the heights of the eternal hills.

Thou shalt draw me out of the snares which they hid for me: for thou art my helper.

Into thy hands, O Lady, I commend my spirit: my whole life and my last day.

Glory be to the Father, etc.

PSALM 31

Blessed are they whose hearts love thee, O Virgin Mary: their sins will be mercifully washed away by thee.

Holy, chaste, and flowering are thy breasts: which blossomed into the flower of eternal greenness.

The beauty of thy grace will never see corruption: and the grace of thy countenance will never fade.

Blessed art thou, O sublime Rod of Jesse: for thou hast raised thyself unto Him who sits in the highest.

O Virgin Queen, thou thyself art the way by which salvation from on high hath visited us.

Glory be to the Father, etc.

PSALM 32

Rejoice, ye just, in the Virgin Mary: and in uprightness of heart praise ye her together.

Draw near unto her with reverence and devotion: and let your heart be delighted in her salutation.

Give unto her the sacrifice of praise: and be ye inebriated from the breasts of her sweetness.

For she sheds upon you the rays of her loving kindness: and she will enlighten you with the splendors of her mercy.

Her fruit is most sweet: it grows ever sweeter in the mouth and the heart of the wise.

Glory be to the Father, etc.

PSALM 33

I will bless Our Lady at all times: and her praise shall never fail in my mouth.

Magnify her with me: all ye who are nourished with the milk and honey of her refreshment.

In dangers and doubts invoke her: and in necessities you will find sweet help and refreshment.

Take example from her conversation: and be zealous to imitate her charity and humility.

Because thou was most humble, O Lady: thou hast induced the Uncreated Word to take flesh from thee.

Glory be to the Father, etc.

PSALM 34

Judge, O Lady, them that harm me: arise against them and avenge my cause.

My soul will rejoice in thee: and I will devoutly exult in thy benefits.

The heavens and the earth are full of thy grace and sweetness: from every side thy kindness surrounds us.

For wherever we may walk: the fruit of thy virginal womb meets us.

Let us run, therefore, dearly beloved, and salute the noble Virgin overflowing with sweetness: that we may rest in the bosom of her sweetness.

Glory be to the Father, etc.

PSALM 35

The unjust man said that he would sin in secret: by thee let him depart from his impious purpose, O Mother of God.

Incline towards us the countenance of God: impel Him to have mercy.

O Lady, in heaven is thy mercy: and thy grace is spread abroad in the earth.

Power and strength are in thy arm: vigor and fortitude in thy right hand.

Blessed be thy empire over the heavens: blessed be thy magnificence upon the earth.

Glory be to the Father, etc.

PSALM 36

Be not angry with the wicked, O Lady: sweeten their fury by thy grace.

O ye religious and cloistered souls, hope in her: confide in her, ye priests and seculars.

Take delight in her praises: and she will grant the petitions of your heart.

Better is a little with her grace: than treasures of silver and precious stones.

Glory be to thee forever, O Queen of Heaven: and never forget us at any time.

Glory be to the Father, etc.

PSALM 37

O Lady, let not the Lord rebuke me in His anger: obtain for us pardon for our sins.

Let all our desire be in thy sight: our hope and our confidence.

My heart is troubled within me: light departs from my interior.

Enlighten with thy brightness my blindness: sweeten with thy sweetness my contrite heart.

Forsake us not, O Lady, Mother of God: let thy grace and thy power be at my right hand.

Glory be to the Father, etc.

PSALM 38

I said: I will keep my ways, O Lady: when by thee the grace of Christ was given to me.

By thy sweetness my soul was melted: my bowels are inflamed by thy love.

Hear my prayer, O Lady, and my supplication: and let mine enemies pine away.

Have mercy on me from Heaven and from the height of thy throne: and permit me not to be troubled in the valley of misery.

Keep my foot, lest it should be injured: and may thy grace be with my end.

Glory be to the Father, etc.

PSALM 39

Expecting, I have expected thy grace: and thou hast done with me according to the multitude of the mercies of thy name.

Thou hast heard my prayers: and thou hast led me out of the den of misery, and from the pit of the enemy.

Manifold and wonderful are thy gifts, O Lady: incomparable are the gifts of thy graces.

Let all those exult and rejoice in thee who love thee: let them who have hated thy name, fall into hell.

Blessed be thou forever, O Lady: forever, world without end.

Glory be to the Father, etc.

PSALM 40

Blessed Mary understandeth concerning the needy and the poor: who remains faithful in her praises.

Lady of the angels, Queen of the world: purify my heart with the fire of love and of thy charity.

Thou art the mother of the illumination of my heart: thou art the nurse who refreshes my mind.

My mouth longs to praise thee: my mind devoutly aspires to venerate thee with ardent affection.

My soul longs to pray to thee: because the whole of my being commends itself to thy guidance and teaching.

Glory be to the Father, etc.

PSALM 41

As the hart longs for the water-brooks, so doth my soul pine for thy love.

For thou art the mother of my life: and the sublime repairer of my flesh.

For thou art the feeder of the Savior of my soul: the beginning and the end of all my salvation.

Hear me, O Lady, let my stains be cleansed: enlighten me, O Lady, that my darkness may be illuminated.

Let my tepidity be enkindled by thy love: let my torpor be expelled by thy grace.

Glory be to the Father, etc.

PSALM 42

Judge me, O Lady, and discern my cause from the perverse nation: from the malignant serpent and the pestiferous dragon deliver me.

Let thy holy fecundity scatter him: let thy blessed virginity bruise his head.

Let thy holy prayers strengthen us against him: let thy merits put to nought his strength.

Send the persecutor of my soul into the abyss: let the infernal pit swallow him alive.

But I and my soul will bless thy name in the land of my captivity: and I will glorify thee forever and ever.

Glory be to the Father, etc.

PSALM 43

O Lady, we have heard with our ears: and our fathers have told it unto us.

For thy merits are ineffable: and thy wonders exceedingly stupendous.

O Lady, innumerable are thy virtues: and inestimable are thy mercies.

Exult, O my soul, and rejoice in her: for many good things are prepared for those who praise her.

Blessed be thou, O Queen of the Heavens and the angels: and let those who praise thy magnificence be blessed by God.

Glory be to the Father, etc.

PSALM 44

My heart hath uttered a good word, Lady: it is sweetened with honey-flowing dew.

By thy sanctity let my sins be purged: by thy integrity may incorruption be bestowed upon me.

By thy virginity may my soul be loved by Christ: and joined to him by the bond of love.

By thy fecundity I, a captive, am redeemed: by thy virginal bringing forth I am delivered from eternal death.

By thy most worthy Son I, a lost one, am restored: and from the exile of misery I am led back to the homeland of beatitude.

Glory be to the Father, etc.

PSALM 45

O Lady, thou art our refuge in all our needs: and a most powerful force bruising and crushing our enemy.

The world is full of thy benefits: they surpass the heavens and penetrate the depths.

By the fullness of thy grace those who were in the abyss rejoice to find themselves liberated.

By the power of thy virginal fecundity, those who were above this world: rejoice to find themselves freed.

By the glorious Son of thy most holy virginity: men are made companions and fellow-citizens of the angels.

Glory be to the Father, etc.

PSALM 46

All ye nations, clap your hands: sing in jubilee to the glorious Virgin.

For she is the gate of life, the door of salvation, and the way of our reconciliation.

The hope of the penitent: the comfort of those that weep: the blessed peace of hearts, and their salvation.

Have mercy on me, O Lady, have mercy on me: for thou art the light and the hope of all who trust in thee.

By thy salutary fecundity let it please thee: that pardon of my sins may be granted unto me.

Glory be to the Father, etc.

PSALM 47

Great art thou, O Lady, and exceedingly to be praised: in the city of the God of Heaven: in the entire Church of His elect.

Thou hast ascended, hymned by the angelic choirs: buoyed by the archangels, crowned with lilies and roses.

Meet her, ye Powers and Principalities: go to welcome her, ye Virtues and Dominations.

Cherubim, and Thrones, and Seraphim, exalt her: and place her at the right hand of the Spouse, her most loving Son.

Oh, with how joyful a soul, with how serene an aspect hast thou received her, O God of angels and men: and given her the principality over every place of thy domination.

Glory be to the Father, etc.

PSALM 48

Hear ye these things, all ye nations: give ear, all ye who desire to enter the kingdom of God.

Honor the Virgin Mary: and ye will find life and perpetual salvation.

Keep thy poor servants, O Lady: join them with a happy union to Christ.

By the fruit of thy womb, refresh and sustain the hunger of thy little ones.

For after thy bringing forth thou hast remained incorrupt: and after thy Son, inviolate.

Glory be to the Father, etc.

PSALM 49

The God of gods hath spoken to Mary: by Gabriel, his messenger, saying: Hail, full of grace, the Lord is with thee: by thee the salvation of the world is repaired.

The Son of the Most High hath greatly desired thy beauty and thy comeliness.

Adorn thy bridal chamber, O Daughter of Sion: prepare to meet thy God.

Thou shalt conceive by the Holy Ghost: who will make thy delivery virginal and joyful.

Glory be to the Father, etc.

PSALM 50

Have mercy on me, O Lady: for thou art called the Mother of Mercy.

And according to thy mercy: cleanse me from all my iniquities.

Pour forth thy grace upon me and withdraw not from me thine accustomed clemency.

For I will confess my sins to thee and I will accuse myself of all my crimes before thee.
Reconcile me to the Fruit of thy womb: and make peace for me with Him who has created me.

Glory be to the Father, etc.

PSALM 51

Why dost thou glory in malice: O malignant serpent and infernal dragon?

Submit thy head to the Woman: by whose power thou art plunged into hell.

Crush him, O Lady, with the foot of thy power: arise and scatter his malice.

Extinguish his might: and reduce his strength to ashes.

That living, we may exult in thy name: and with joyful soul we may give praise to thee.

Glory be to the Father, etc.

PSALM 52

The foolish enemy hath said in his soul: I will cast men out from the tabernacle of the sons of God.

I will go forth, and I will be a lying spirit in the mouth of the serpent: and by the woman I will cast out the man, her husband.

O wretched one, as the heavens are exalted above the earth: so are the thoughts of God above thy thoughts.

Be not lifted up because of the woman's fall: for it is a woman who shall crush thy head.

Thou hast prepared a pit for her: and in her snare thou shalt be caught.

Glory be to the Father, etc.

PSALM 53

O Lady, save me in thy name: and deliver me from my injustices.

That the craft of the enemy may not hurt me: hide me under the shadow of thy wings.

O my Lady, help me! Bestow thy grace upon my soul!

Willingly I will offer thee a sacrifice of praise: and I will give praise to thy name, for it is good.

For thou shalt deliver me from all tribulation: and my eye shall despise mine enemies.

Glory be to the Father, etc.

PSALM 54

Hear my prayer, O Lady: and do not despise my supplications.

I am become sad in my thoughts: because the judgments of God have terrified me.

The darkness of death has overtaken me: and the fear of hell has invaded me.

But in solitude I will expect thy consolation: and in my chamber I will wait for thy mercy.

Glorify thy arm and thy right hand: that our enemies may be prostrated by us.

Glory be to the Father, etc.

PSALM 55

Have mercy on me, O Lady, for my enemies have trodden upon me every day: all their thoughts are turned to evil against me.

Stir up fury, and be mindful of war: and pour out thy anger upon them.

Renew wonders and change marvelous things: let us feel the help of thine arm.

Glorify thy name upon us: that we may know that thy mercy is forever.

Distill upon us the drops of thy sweetness: for thou art the cupbearer of the sweetness of grace.

Glory be to the Father, etc.

PSALM 56

Have mercy on me, O Lady, have mercy on me: for my heart is prepared to seek out thy will.

And I will rest in the shelter of thine arms: for sweet to me is thy refreshment.

Thy hands have distilled the first myrrh: and thy fingers the unguents of graces.

And a fragment of pomegranate is thy throat: and thy breath is sweet as an amalgam of choice smelling herbs.

For thou art the mother of fair love and the anchor of hope: the harbor of safety, indulgence or pardon, and the gate of salvation.

Glory be to the Father, etc.

PSALM 57

If indeed you will truly speak justice: honor the Queen of justice and mercy.

For this belongs to the praise and the glory of the Savior: whatever of honor is bestowed upon the Mother.

The roses of martyrs surround thee, O Queen: and the lilies of virgins encompass thy throne.

Praise ye her, all together, ye morning stars: the seas and the rivers and the foundations of the world.

Glory be to the Father, etc.

PSALM 58

Deliver me from mine enemies, O Lady of the world: arise to meet me, O Queen of piety.

The purest gold is thy ornament: the sardine stone and the topaz are thy diadem.

The jasper and the amethyst are in thy right hand: the beryl and the chrysolite in thy left.

The hyacinths are on thy breast: shining carbuncles are the jewels of thy bracelets.

Myrrh, frankincense, and balsam are on thy hands: the sapphire and the emerald on thy fingers.

Glory be to the Father, etc.

PSALM 59

O God, thou hast cast us off because of our sins: thou hast had mercy on us by the Virgin Mary.

Intercede for us, O saving Mother of God: who hast brought forth salvation for men and angels.

For thou infuses joy into the sad: and joy and sweetness into the mourners.

Rejoice us by the sweet sounds of thy speech: and pour thy balm of roses forth into our hearts.

Thunder, ye heavens, from above, and give praise to her: glorify her, ye earth, with all the dwellers therein.

Glory be to the Father, etc.

PSALM 60

Hear my prayer, O Lady: upon a firm rock establish my mind.

Be thou to me a tower of strength: protect me from the face of the cruel destroyer.

Be thou to him terrible as an army in battle array: and may he fall living into the depths of hell.

For thou art shining and terrible: a cloud full of dew, and the rising dawn.

Thou art beautiful and bright as the full moon: thy sacred aspect is as when the sun shines in its strength.

Glory be to the Father, etc.

PSALM 61

O Lady, shall not my soul be subject to thee: who hast brought forth the Savior of all?

Be mindful of us, O savior of the lost: hear thou the weeping of our hearts.

Pour forth graces from thy treasury: and with thine unguents soothe our grief.

Give us joy and peace: that thou mayest confound the enemies of the good.

Wash away all our sins: heal all our infirmities.

Glory be to the Father, etc.

PSALM 62

O God, my God: I will glorify thee by Thy Mother.

For she hath conceived thee in virginity: and without travail she hath brought Thee forth.

Blessed be thou, O Lady: stand for us before the throne of God.

Beauty and brightness are in thy sight.

Keep my soul, O Lady: that it may never fall into sin.

Glory be to the Father, etc.

PSALM 63

Hear my prayer, O Lady, when I beseech thee: from the fear of the cruel one deliver my soul.

Obtain for us peace and salvation: in the last day.

Blessed be thou above all women: and blessed be the fruit of thy womb.

Enlighten, O Lady, mine eyes: and illumine my blindness.

Give me firm confidence in thee: in my life and in mine end.

Glory be to the Father, etc.

PSALM 64

A hymn becometh thee, O Lady, in Sion: praise and jubilation in Jerusalem.

The Lord hath given thee the blessing of all nations: praise and glory in the sight of all peoples.

The Lord hath blessed thee in His mercy: and hath set thy throne above all the orders of angels.

He hath placed grace and beauty in thy lips: and with a mantle of glory he hath clothed thy body.

He hath set a resplendent crown upon thy head: and hath adorned thee with the jewels of virtues.

Glory be to the Father, etc.

PSALM 65

Shout with joy to Our Lady, all the earth: sing ye a psalm to her name: give honor to her majesty.

Blessed be thy heart, O Lady: with which thou hast ardently and sincerely loved the Son of God.

Look upon my poverty, O glorious Virgin: delay not to remove my misery and my difficulties.

Take away my tribulations: sweeten my weariness.

Let all flesh bless thee: let every tongue glorify thee.

Glory be to the Father, etc.

PSALM 66

May God have mercy on us and bless us: by her who brought Him forth.

Have mercy on us, O Lady, and pray for us: turn our sadness into joy.

Enlighten me, O Star of the sea: shed thy brightness upon me, O resplendent Virgin.

Extinguish the burning of my heart: refresh me with thy grace.

Let thy grace ever protect me: let thy presence give light to my end.

Glory be to the Father, etc.

PSALM 67

Let Mary arise, and let her enemies be scattered: let them all be crushed beneath her feet.

Break thou the attack of our enemies: destroy all their iniquity.

To thee, O Lady, have I cried in my tribulation: and thou hast given serenity to my conscience.

Let not thy praise fail in our mouths: nor thy love in our hearts.

There is much peace to them that love thee, O Lady: their souls shall not see death forever.

Glory be to the Father, etc.

PSALM 68

Save me, O Lady: for the waters of concupiscence have entered into my very soul.

I am stuck fast in the mire of sin: and the waters of pleasure have encompassed me.

Weeping, I have wept in the night: and the day of joy has arisen for me.

Save my soul, O Mother of the Savior: for by thee true salvation was given to the world.

While thou was overshadowed when the Angel spoke to thee: and became pregnant with the Wisdom of the Father.

Glory be to the Father, etc.

PSALM 69

O Lady, come to my assistance: and by the light of thy mercy enlighten me.

Teach us to seek thy goodness: that we may declare thy wonders.

Show forth thy power against our enemies: that thou mayest be praised among the distant nations.

In the flames of thy wrath let them be plunged into hell: and may they who trouble thy servants find perdition.

Have mercy on thy servants, upon whom thy name is invoked: and do not permit them to be straitened in their temptations.

Glory be to the Father, etc.

PSALM 70

In thee, O Lady, have I hoped: let me never be confounded: in thy mercy deliver me and free me.

Because of the multitude of my iniquities: I am vehemently oppressed.

Mine enemies have acted above my head: they have mocked me and derided me day by day.

See, O Lady, how I am troubled: stretch forth thy hands, and succor him who perishes.

Delay not, for the sake of the grace of thy name: and thou shalt become unto me joy and salvation.

Glory be to the Father, etc.

PSALM 71

Give to the King thy judgment, O God: and thy mercy to the Queen, His Mother.

In thy hand are life and salvation: perpetual joy and glorious eternity.

Sprinkle my heart with thy sweetness: make me forget the miseries of this life.

Draw me after thee by the bands of thy mercy: and with the bandages of thy grace and loving kindness heal my pain.

Stir up in me a desire for Heaven: and inebriate my soul with the joy of Paradise.

Glory be to the Father, etc.

PSALM 72

How good is God to Israel: to those who pay homage to His Mother and venerate her.

For she is our comfort: she is the most excellent of help in labor.

The enemy hath overspread my soul with darkness: O Lady, make light arise within me.

Let the wrath of God be turned away from me by thee: placate him by thy merits and thy prayers.

Stand for me in the Day of Judgment: in His presence take up my cause, and be my advocate.

Glory be to the Father, etc.

PSALM 73

O Lady, why hast thou cast us off? and why wilt thou not help us in the day of tribulation?

Let my prayer come into thy sight: and despise not the voices of those who groan.

The enemy hath stretched his bow against us: he has strengthened his right hand, and there is no consoler.

Break for us the bonds of his malicious doings: and deliver us by thy right hand.

Drive him back into the place of perdition: let eternal damnation possess him.

Glory be to the Father, etc.

PSALM 74

We will praise thee, O Lady: and we will praise thy name: make us to delight in thy praises.

Sing ye to her, ye dwellers upon earth: and announce her praise to the peoples.

Praise and magnificence are before her: fortitude and exultation are in her throne.

Adore ye her in her beauty: glorify the Maker of her beauty.

Be mindful in eternity of her mercy: keep in mind her virtues and her wonders.

Glory be to the Father, etc.

PSALM 75

In Judea God is known: in Israel the honor of His Mother.

Sweet is the memory of her above honey and the honeycomb: and her love is above all aromatic perfumes.

Health and life are in her house: and in her dwelling are peace and eternal glory.

Honor her, ye heavens and earth: because the supreme artificer has wonderfully honored her.

Give to her praise, all ye creatures: and joyfully celebrate her astonishing mercy.

Glory be to the Father, etc.

PSALM 76

With my voice I cried to the Lady: and by her grace she bowed down to me.

She hath taken sorrow and grief from my heart: and she hath soothed my heart by her sweetness.

She hath turned my fear into a sweet confidence: and by her honey-flowing aspect she hath calmed my mind.

By her holy help I have avoided the dangers of death: and I have escaped the cruel hand.

Thanks be to God and to thee, O loving Mother, for all things which I have obtained: for thy piety and thy mercy.

Glory be to the Father, etc.

PSALM 77

Attend, O people of God, to His commandments: and forget not the Queen of grace.

Open your heart to search her out: and your lips to glorify her.

Let her love come down into your hearts: long to please her.

Her beauty outshines the sun and the moon: she is adorned with the ornaments of virtues.

Have mercy on me, O Queen of glory and honor: and keep my soul from all danger.

Glory be to the Father, etc.

PSALM 78

O Lady, the heathen have come into the inheritance of God: which thou hast established in Christ by thy merits.

Let thy speech be sweet before Him: and unite me to Him who hath redeemed me.

Stretch forth thine arm against the cruel enemy: and unfold to me his craft.

Thy voice is sweet above every melody: the angelic harmony cannot be compared with it.

Drop down on me the sweetness of thy graces: and the fragrance of thy heavenly gifts.

Glory be to the Father, etc.

PSALM 79

Give ear to me, thou who rulest Israel: praise thy Mother with me.

Arise and shake thyself from the dust, O my soul: go forth to meet the Queen of Heaven.

Loose the bands of thy neck, O poor little soul of mine: and welcome her with glorious praises.

The odor of life comes forth from her: and all salvation springs out of her heart.

By the sweet fragrance of her spiritual gifts: dead souls are raised to life.

Glory be to the Father, etc.

PSALM 80

Rejoice to the Lady, our helper: sing aloud in the joy of your heart.

Let your affections be enkindled in her: and she will overwhelm your enemies with confusion.

Let us imitate her humility: her obedience and her meekness.

All graces shine forth in her: for her capacity was immense.

Run ye to her with holy devotion: and she will share her good things with you.

Glory be to the Father, etc.

PSALM 81

God is in the congregation of Jews: from whom, as a rose, has come forth the Mother of God.

Wipe away my stains, O Lady: thou who art ever resplendent in purity.

Make the fountain of life flow into my mouth: whence the living waters take their rise and flow forth.

All ye who thirst, come to her: she will willingly give you to drink from her fountain.

He who drinketh from her, will spring forth unto life everlasting: and he will never thirst.

Glory be to the Father etc.

PSALM 82

O my Lady, who shall be like unto thee? In grace and glory thou surpassest all.

As the heavens are above the earth: so art thou high above all, and exceedingly exalted.

Wound my heart with thy charity: make me worthy of thy grace and thy gifts.

May my heart melt in thy fear: and may the desire of thee enkindle my soul.

Make me desire thy honor and thy glory: that I may be received by thee into the peace of Jesus Christ.

Glory be to the Father, etc.

PSALM 83

How lovely are thy tabernacles, O Lady of hosts: how delightful are the tents of thy redemption.

Honor her, O ye sinners: and she will obtain grace and salvation for you.

Her prayer is incense above frank-incense and balsam: her supplications will not return to her bare, void, or empty.

Intercede for me, O Lady, with thy Christ: neither do thou forsake me in death or in life.

For thy spirit is kind: thy grace fills the whole world.

Glory be to the Father, etc.

PSALM 84

O Lady, thou hast blessed thy house: thou hast consecrated thy dwelling.

This one is fair among the daughters of Jerusalem: whose memory is in blessing.

The holy angels have proclaimed her blessed: glorify her, ye Virtues and Dominations.

Ye peoples and nations, seek out her prudence: and search out the treasures of her mercy.

Think of her in goodness: and seek her in simplicity of heart.

Glory be to the Father, etc.

PSALM 85

Incline thine ear, O Lady, and hear me: turn thy face to me, and have mercy on me.

May the inflowing of thy sweetness delight the souls of the saints: and the infusion of thy charity be sweet above the sweetest honey.

The resplendence of thy glory enlightens the mind: and the light of thy mercies leads to salvation.

The fountain of thy goodness inebriates the thirsty: and the aspect of thy countenance draws men away from sin.

To know thee and to learn thee is the root of immortality: and to declare thy virtues is the way of salvation.

Glory be to the Father, etc.

PSALM 86

The foundations of life in the soul of the just: are to persevere in charity unto the end.

Thy grace raises up the poor man in adversity: and the invocation of thy name inspires him with confidence.

Paradise is filled with thy tender mercies: and by the fear of thee the infernal enemy is confounded.

He who hopes in thee, will find treasures of peace: and he who invokes thee not in this life, will not attain to the kingdom of God.

Grant, O Lady, that we may live in the grace of the Holy Ghost: and lead our souls to a holy end.

Glory be to the Father, etc.

PSALM 87

Lady, thou art the helper of my salvation: by day and by night I have cried to thee.

Let my prayer enter into thy sight: console my sadness with the sight of thee.

Evils are multiplied in my soul: cleanse it from filth and sin.

May thy power overcome our enemies: lest they hinder our salvation.

Bestow on us thy grace to resist them: strengthen our hearts against the concupiscence of the flesh.

Glory be to the Father, etc.

PSALM 88

Thy mercies, O Lady, I will sing forever.

With the ointment of thy tender mercy heal the broken in heart: and with the oil of thy mercy console our griefs.

May thy gracious countenance appear to me in my end: may the beauty of thy face rejoice my spirit in its going forth.

Stir up my spirit to love thy goodness: excite my mind to extol thy nobility and worth.

Deliver me from evil and tribulation: and from all sin keep thou my soul.

Glory be to the Father, etc

PSALM 89

O Lady, thou art made unto us refreshment: in all our needs.

The diffusion of thy grace produces thy holy operations in us: and the gentle dropping of thy sweetness maketh holy affections.

I will be mindful, O Lady, of thy tender mercies: I will sing unto thee a sacrifice of praise and a song of joy.

They who honor thee will obtain a perennial crown for ashes: and the mantle of praise for the spirit of mourning.

They who hope in thee will be clothed with light: joy and perpetual rejoicing will be their lot.

Glory be to the Father. etc.

PSALM 90

He that dwells in the help of the Mother of God: will abide under her protection.

The concourse of enemies will not harm him: the flying arrow will not touch him.

For she will deliver him from the snare of the hunter: and under her wings she will protect him.

Cry out to her in your dangers: and the scourge will not come nigh your dwelling.

He who has placed his hope in her, will find the fruit of grace: the gate of paradise will be opened to him.

Glory be to the Father, etc.

PSALM 91

It is good to give praise to the Virgin Mary: and to sing glory to her is the prosperity of the mind.

To declare her merits rejoices the mind: and to imitate her works makes glad the angels of God.

He who obtains her favor: is recognized by the dwellers in Paradise.

And he who shall bear the character of her name, shall be written in the book of life.

Arise, O Lady, and judge our cause: and deliver us from those who rise up against us.

Withdraw not thy right hand from the sinner: and meet with thy sword the darts of the destroyer.

Glory be to the Father, etc.

PSALM 92

The Lord hath reigned, He is clothed with beauty: He hath crowned His Mother with the ornaments of virtues.

May the Mother of peace fulfill in us his propitiation: and may she teach her servants the way of equity.

Ye who desire the wisdom of Christ: serve His Mother with a reverent soul.

Who will suffice to relate thy works, O Lady? And who shall search out the treasures of thy mercy?

Do thou uphold those who are fainting away in their temptations: and appoint them a lot in truth.

Glory be to the Father, etc.

PSALM 93

The Lord is a God to whom revenge belongs: but thou, O Mother of mercy, inclinest Him to mercy.

Thy magnificence, O Lady, is preached forever: and they who venerate thee shall find the way of peace.

Serve her reverently with rejoicing: and the Most Blessed Fruit of her womb shall heal you.

Look, O Lady, upon the humility of thy servants: and they shall praise thee in the generations of ages.

Magnify thy name in the multiplication of thy graces: and permit not thy servants to be subject to perils.

Glory be to the Father, etc.

PSALM 94

Come, let us rejoice to Our Lady: let us joyfully sing to the saving Mary, our Queen.

Let us come before her presence with joy: and in canticles let us all praise her together.

Come, let us adore, and fall down before her: let us confess our sins to her with tears.

Obtain for us a full pardon, stand for us before the tribunal of God.

Receive our souls at our end: and lead us into eternal rest.

Glory be to the Father, etc.

ing a new song to her who is full of grace: sing to Mary all ye of the
arthly world.

or she excels in sanctity all the angels: and those born of women in her
wonders and miracles.

Beauty and glory are in her countenance: and grace is in her eyes.

Bring ye to her glory, ye fathers o$ the peoples: rejoice in her, all ye crea-
ures of God.

You have an admirable exchange worked by her means: by reason of which
ou are called the sons of the Most High God.

Glory be to the Father, etc.

PSALM 96

The Lord hath reigned, let Mary rejoice: in all the empire under her rule.

Adore her, all ye citizens of the heavenly commonwealth: exalt her; ye fair
virgins, her daughters.

For she is raised above principalities and dominations: she is exalted above
angels and the embassies of archangels.

Patriarchs and prophets, break forth in her praise: make a harmony, Apostles
and martyrs of Christ.

Confessors and virgins, sing canticles to her from the songs of Sion: and
congratulate her, holy monks, for the triumphs she has won.

Glory be to the Father, etc.

PSALM 97

Sing to Our Lady a new song: for she hath done wonderful things.

In the sight of nations she hath revealed her mercy: her name is heard even to the ends of the earth.

Be mindful, O Lady, of the poor and the wretched: and support them by the help of thy holy refreshment.

For thou, O Lady, art sweet and true: exceedingly patient and full of compassion.

Tread upon the enemies of our souls: and crush with thy holy arm their contumacy.

Glory be to the Father, etc.

PSALM 98

The Lord hath reigned, let the people be angry: Mary sits at the right hand under the Cherubim.

Great in Sion is thy glory, O Lady: and in Jerusalem thy magnificence.

Sing before her, ye virginal choirs: and adore her throne, for it is holy.

In her right hand is the fiery law: and round about her are millions of saints.

Her commands are before his eyes: and the rule of justice is in her heart.

Glory be to the Father, etc.

PSALM 99

ing with joy to Our Lady, ye men of the earth: serve her in joy and pleasantness.

With all your soul draw nigh unto her: and in all your strength keep her ways.

Search her out, and she will be manifested to you: be clean of heart, and you will take hold of her.

To them whom thou shalt help, O Lady, will be the refreshment of peace: and they from whom thou turns away thy face shall have no hope of salvation.

Be mindful of us, O Lady, and let evil not take hold of us: help us in the end, and we shall find eternal life.

Glory be to the Father, etc.

PSALM 100

To thee, O Lady, will I sing mercy and judgment: I will sing to thee in joy of heart, when thou shalt have made my soul glad.

I will praise thee and thy glory: and thou shalt bestow refreshment upon my soul.

I have been zealous for thy love and thy honor: therefore wilt thou defend my cause before the judge of ages.

I am drawn by thy goodness and grace: I pray thee, let me not be defrauded of my hope and good confidence.

Strengthen thou my soul in my last days: and in this my flesh make me to behold my Savior.

Glory be to the Father, etc.

PSALM 101

O Lady, hear my prayer: and let my cry come unto thee.

Turn not thy sacred countenance away from me: nor hate me because of my uncleanness.

Forsake me not in the thought and counsel of mine enemies: and permit me not to fall in their wicked attacks.

Those who trust in thee, will not fear the tortuous snake: and those who exalt thee in praises will escape the hand of Acheron.

By thy virginal conception give me a good confidence in thee: and by thy admirable delivery rejoice my soul.

Glory be to the Father, etc.

PSALM 102

Bless, O my soul, the Mother of Jesus Christ: and all that is within me, glorify her name.

Forget not her benefits: nor her grace and consolation.

By her grace sins are forgiven: and by her mercy maladies are healed.

Bless her, all ye powers of Heaven: glorify her, ye choirs of the Apostles and Prophets.

Bless her, O ye sea, and the islands of the nations: sing a hymn to her, all ye heavens and the dwellers therein.

Glory be to the Father, etc.

PSALM 103

Bless, O my soul, the Virgin Mary: her honor and her magnificence forever.

Thou hast clothed thyself with beauty and comeliness: thou art clad, O Lady, with a shining garment.

From thee proceeds the healing of sins: and the discipline of peace, and the fervor of charity.

Fill us, thy servants, with holy virtues: and let the wrath of God not come nigh unto us.

Give eternal joy to thy servants: and forget them not in the death struggle.

Glory be to the Father, etc.

PSALM 104

Give praise to Our Lady and call upon her name: sing gloriously unto her, declaring her virtues.

Praise and exalt her, O Virgins, daughters of Sion: because she will espouse to you the King of Angels.

Honor ye the Queen full of all grace: and contemplate with reverence her most holy countenance.

Eternal salvation is in thy hand, O Lady: those who honor thee worthily will receive it.

Thy clemency will not fail in the eternal years: and thy mercy is from generation to generation.

Glory be to the Father, etc.

PSALM 105

Give praise to Our Lady, for she is good: in all the tribes of the earth relate her mercies.

Far from the impious is her conversation: her foot has not declined from the way of the Most High.

A fountain of fertilizing grace comes forth from her mouth: and a virginal emanation sanctifying chaste souls.

The hope of the glory of Paradise is in her heart: for the devout soul who shall have honored her.

Have mercy on us, O resplendent Queen of Heaven: and give consolation from thy glory.

Glory be to the Father, etc.

PSALM 106

Give praise to the Lord, for He is good: give praise to His Mother, for her mercy endureth for ever.

Show us, O Lady, the innocence and the way of prudence: and point out the way of understanding to thy servants.

The fear of God enlightens the mind: and thy love rejoices it.

Blessed is the man whose speech is pleasing to thee: his bones shall be fattened with marrow and fatness.

Thy word shall uphold the feeble soul: and thy lips shall refresh the thirsty soul.

Glory be to the Father, etc.

PSALM 107

My heart is ready, O Lady, my heart is ready: to sing praises to thee and to chant.

Greater is thy love than all riches: and thy grace is above gold and precious stones.

Beatitude and justice are given by God: for those who turn away from their sins to thee shall obtain the remedy of penance.

Thy fruits are grace and peace: and those who please thee shall be far from perdition.

Be to us a shade of protection in our temptations: let the spreading of thy wings defend us from him who devours.

Glory be to the Father, etc.

PSALM 108

O Lady, despise not my praise: and deign to accept this Psalter dedicated to thee.

Look upon the will of my heart: and make my affection well-pleasing to thee.

Hasten to visit thy servants: under the protection of thy hand may they be preserved unhurt.

May they receive through thee the illumination of the Holy Spirit: and refreshment against the heat of cupidity.

Heal, O Lady, the contrite of heart: and revive them by the ointment of piety.

Glory be to the Father, etc.

PSALM 109

The Lord said to Our Lady: Sit at my right hand, O my Mother!

Goodness and sanctity have pleased thee: therefore thou shalt reign with me forever.

The crown of immortality is on thy holy head: whose brightness and glory shall not be extinguished.

Have mercy on us, O Lady, mother of light and splendor: enlighten us, O Lady of truth and virtue.

From thy treasures pour into us the wisdom of God: and the understanding of prudence, and the model of discipline.

Glory be to the Father, etc.

PSALM 110

I will give praise to thee, O Lady, with my whole soul: I will glorify thee with my whole mind.

The works of thy grace will remain: and the testament of thy mercy before the throne of God.

By thee redemption has been sent from God: the repentant people shall have the hope of salvation.

A good understanding to all who honor thee: and their lot is among the angels of peace.

Glorious and admirable is thy name: those who keep it will not fear in the moment of death.

Glory be to the Father, etc.

PSALM 111

Blessed is the man who feareth the Lady: and blessed is the heart that loves her.

Happy the man who is never satiated with thy praise: and grows not weary of the narration of thy virtues.

In his heart has arisen the light of God: the Holy Spirit enlightens his understanding.

Bestow, O Lady, thy grace upon thy poor: revive the hungry and the needy.

By thee names shall be in eternal remembrance: our heart shall not fear the evil hearing.

Glory be to the Father, etc.

PSALM 112

Praise, ye children, the Mother of God: ye old men, glorify her name.

Blessed be Mary, the Mother of Christ: for she is the way to the homeland of sanctity.

Her throne is high above the Cherubim: her throne is above the hinges of heaven.

Her countenance is upon the humble: and her looks upon those who trust in her.

Her mercy is over all flesh: and her almsgiving until the ends of the earth.

Glory be to the Father, etc.

PSALM 113

In the going forth of my soul from this world: meet it, O Lady, and receive it.

Console it with thy holy countenance: let not the sight of the demons terrify it.

Be to it a ladder to Heaven: and a straight way to the Paradise of God.

Obtain for it from the Father the pardon of peace: and a throne of light among the servants of God.

Uphold the devout before the tribunal of Christ: take their cause into thy hands.

Glory be to the Father, etc.

PSALM 114

I have loved the Mother of the Lord my God: and the light of her compassions she hath shined upon me.

The sorrows of death have encompassed me: and the visitation of Mary hath rejoiced me.

I have incurred grief and danger: and I have been recreated by her grace.

Let her name and her memory be in the midst of our heart: and the blow of the malignant will not injure us.

Be converted, my soul, unto her praise: and thou shalt find refreshment in thy last end.

Glory be to the Father, etc.

believed, therefore I have spoken: thy glory, O Lady, to the whole world.

Have compassion on my soul, and guide it: deign in thy good pleasure to take possession of it.

Assign to it the testament of thy peace and thy love: give to it the memory of thy name.

Of the blessing of thy womb give me support: and from the fatness of thy grace sweeten my soul. Break thou the bonds of my sins: and with thy virtues adorn the face of my soul.

Glory be to the Father, etc.

PSALM 116

Praise ye our Lady, all ye nations: glorify her, all ye peoples.

For her grace and her mercy are confirmed upon us: and her truth remaineth forever.

He who shall worthily have venerated her, will be justified: but he who shall have neglected her, will die in his sins.

The lips of angels shall relate her wisdom: and all the citizens of Paradise will sing her praises.

Those who approach her with a good soul: will not be seized by the devastating angel.

Glory be to the Father, etc.

PSALM 117

Give praise to the Lord, for He is good: give praise to His Mother, for her mercy endureth forever.

The love of her drives out sin from the heart: and her grace purifies the conscience of the sinner.

The way to come to Christ is to approach her: he who shall fly her shall not find the way of Peace.

Let him who is hardened in sins, often call upon her: and light shall arise in his darkness.

He who is sad in his heart, let him cry out to her: and he will be inebriated with a sweet-flowing dew.

Glory be to the Father, etc.

PSALM 118

Blessed are the undefiled in the way: who imitate the Mother of God.

Blessed are the imitators of her humility: blessed are the sharers in her charity.

Blessed are the searchers into her virtues: blessed are they who are conformed to her image.

Blessed are they who venerate her conception and her birth: blessed are they who devoutly serve her.

Blessed are they who have hope and confidence in her: blessed are they who receive through her eternal happiness.

Glory be to the Father, etc.

PSALM 118A

Give bountifully to thy servant, O Lady: enliven me, and I shall do thy will.

I am a sojourner on the earth: hide nothing of thy love from me.

My soul hath longed to desire thy praise: at all times.

For thou art my salvation in the Lord: who hast delivered me, one condemned to death.

What shall I give back for these things, except my whole self? O Lady receive me.

Glory be to the Father, etc.

PSALM 118B

Set before me for a law, O Lady, the holy of holies of thy will: and I shall always seek after it.

Lead me into the path of thy tender mercies, O most beautiful of women: for this same have I desired.

Incline my soul to the love of those above, O Lady: and not to unchasteness.

Behold I have coveted thy chastity from my youth up: in thy mercy strengthen me.

And I will keep the way of thy testimonies forever: and I will search out the commandments of thy Son, which I have loved.

Glory be to the Father, etc.

PSALM 118C

Be mindful of thy word, O Princess of all ladies: in which thou hast given me hope.

In the stormy waves of tempests it hath powerfully held me: for thy word hath quickened me.

Lying men have surrounded me, and scourges are gathered together upon me: and behold thy hand hath delivered me.

I have communicated all good things to them that fear thee: and to those who earnestly kept thy commandments.

The earth is full of thy tender mercies: therefore, have I sought out the way of thy justifications.

Glory be to the Father, etc.

PSALM 118D

Thou hast done well with thy servant, O Lady: and because of this the angels rejoice.

Teach me the discipline of thy manners and thy equity: because I have believed in thy words above all others.

It is good for me that with thy burden thou hast humbled me: that I may follow thy conversation.

Those who love thy servants, shall be venerated: but he who shall hate them will fall in eternity.

Let the drops of thy clemency ever fall upon me from above, and I shall live for thy holy law is my meditation.

Glory be to the Father, etc.

PSALM 118E

My soul hath fainted in thy ways, O Lady: and unless thou didst have the greatest compassion on me, I should indeed have perished in my weakness.

My eyes have failed in thy contemplation: like a bottle in the frost my soul has been before thee.

According to thy goodness quicken thou me: and I shall not forget thy words, because to cling to thee is good.

By thy ruling the world goes on: which thou together with God hast founded from the beginning.

I am all thine, o Lady; save me: for thy praises were desirable to me in the time of my pilgrimage.

Glory be to the Father, etc.

PSALM 118F

How have I loved thy law, O Lady: it is forever in my sight.

The abundance of thy sweetnesses has drawn my heart out of me: and my flesh hath wonderfully rejoiced in thee.

How sweet to sinners are thy words, O Lady: above all melody thy refection is sweet to my mouth.

Thy word is a light to my steps: and an ineffable illumination to my paths.

How often have sinners of hell exasperated me, because I would not stray from thy charity: but in thee, O Lady have I hoped.

Glory be to the Father, etc.

PSALM 118G

I have hated the unjust: and I have loved thy way, O gracious Lady.

Help me, O Lady of the world, and I shall be saved: and I shall meditate the honor of thy commandments.

Make me always stand in thy fear: and deliver me not up, O Virgin, to those who calumniate me.

I am of thy own tongue: I am the least in thy family.

Keep me, O Lady, from those who neglect the judgments of thy justice.

Thou despisest all who depart from thy service: because their thought is unjust.

Glory be to the Father, etc.

PSALM 118H

Wonderful are thy testimonies, O kind Mother: and by thy words my heart is enlightened.

All the rich of the people shall entreat thy countenance: and the daughters of kings shall praise thy face.

The word of thy lips is burning exceedingly: He who shall make haste to come to thee, shall share in it.

I am as a trembling reed before thee: hold me, Lady, under thy yoke, and I shall not be confounded.

The dragons of hell attack thy servants above all others: but do thou, O Lady, defend us.

Glory be to the Father, etc.

have cried out to thee with my whole heart, O Lady: mercifully deliver me from my necessities.

Hear the voice of my groaning, O my Lady: teach me what is acceptable to thee at all times.

Salvation is far from those who know thee not: but he who perseveres in thy service is far from perdition.

Thy mercy rules all things: O Lady, in thy salvation quicken me.

The beginning of thy words is truth at all times: and I have not forgotten thine immaculate law.

Glory be to the Father, etc.

PSALM 118J

Princes have persecuted me without cause: and the wicked spirit fears the invocation of thy name.

There is much peace to them that keep thy name, O Mother of God: and to them there is no stumbling-block.

At the seven hours I have sung praises to thee, O Lady: according to thy word give me understanding.

Let my prayer come into thy sight, that I may not forsake thee, O Lady, all the days of my life: for thy ways are mercy and truth.

I will long forever to praise thee, O Lady: when thou shalt have taught me thy justifications.

Glory be to the Father, etc.

PSALM 119

I cried to Our Lady when I was in trouble: and she heard me.

Lady, deliver us from all evil: all the days of our life.

Crush the head of our enemies: with the insuperable power of thy foot.

As thy spirit hath rejoiced in God thy Savior: so do thou deign to pour true joy into my heart.

Approach to Our Lord to pray for us: that by thee our sins may be blotted out.

Glory be to the Father, etc.

PSALM 120

To thee I have raised mine eyes, O Mother of Christ: by whom comfort cometh to all flesh.

Bestow on us thy help and thy grace: in all our tribulations.

Keep us, O Lady: lest we be caught in the snare of sinners.

The pupil of thine eye neither slumbers nor sleeps: that we may always be kept under thy protection.

The tongues of men and angels praise thee: and before thee every knee shall bow.

Glory be to the Father, etc.

PSALM 121

rejoiced in thee, O Queen of Heaven: because under thy leadership we shall go into the house of the Lord.

Jerusalem the heavenly city: may we attain to the rewards of Mary.

Obtain for us, O Lady, peace and pardon: and the victory over our enemies, and triumph.

Strengthen and console our hearts: by the sweetness of thy piety.

Do, Lady, pour into us thy mercy: that we may devoutly die in the Lord.

Glory be to the Father, etc.

PSALM 122

To thee have I raised up mine eyes, O Queen: who reignest in Heaven.

Let our help be in the power of thy name: let all our works be directed by thee.

Blessed be thou in Heaven and on earth: in the sea and in all abysses.

Blessed be thy fecundity: blessed be thy virginity and purity.

Blessed be thy holy body: blessed be thy most holy soul.

Glory be to the Father, etc.

PSALM 123

Unless our Lady was in us: many dangers would have overtaken us.

O Virgin, be our defender: and a propitious advocate before God.

Show us, O Lady, thy mercy: and strengthen us in thy holy service.

Let the holy angels bless thee in Heaven: let all men bless thee upon earth.

Give not up to the beasts the souls of them that trust in thee: let not the mouths of them that sing to thee be closed.

Glory be to the Father, etc.

PSALM 124

Those who trust in thee, O Mother of God: shall not fear at the face of the enemy.

Rejoice and exult, all ye who love her: because she will help you in the day of your trouble.

Be mindful of thy tender mercies, O Lady: and relieve us in the pilgrimage of our sojourning.

Turn thine amiable countenance towards us: confound and destroy all our enemies.

Blessed be all the works of thy hands, O Lady: blessed be all thy holy miracles.

Glory be to the Father, etc.

PSALM 125

When thou shalt turn thy most serene countenance upon us: thou shalt rejoice us, O virginal Mother of God.

Blessed be thou, O treasury of Christ: above all women upon earth.

Blessed be thy glorious name: which the mouth of the Lord hath wonderfully named.

Let not thy praise fail from our lips: nor thy charity from our hearts.

Those who love thee will be blessed by God: and those who wish to love thee, will not be defrauded of their confidence.

Glory be to the Father, etc.

PSALM 126

Unless, O Lady, thou shalt build the house of our heart: its edifice shall not remain.

Build us up by thy grace and thy power: that we may remain firm forever.

Blessed be thy word: and blessed be all the words of thy lips.

Let them be blessed by God, who shall bless thee: and let them be reckoned in the number of the just. Bless, O Lady, them that bless thee: and never turn thy gracious countenance away from them.

Glory be to the Father, etc.

PSALM 127

Blessed are all they who fear our Lady: and blessed are all they who know how to do thy will and thy good pleasure.

Blessed are the father and mother who have begotten thee: whose memory shall abide forever.

Blessed is the womb that bore thee: and blessed are the breasts that nourished thee.

Turn thou thy mercy toward us: and be gracious to thy servants.

Look upon us and behold our shame: take away from us all our iniquities.

Glory be to the Father, etc.

PSALM 128

My enemies have often troubled me from my youth up: deliver me, O Lady, and vindicate my cause from them.

Give them not power over my soul: keep my interior and my exterior.

Obtain for us pardon for our sins: let it be given to us by the grace of the Holy Spirit.

Make us do penance worthily and praiseworthily: that we may come to God by a blessed end.

Show us then with a gracious and serene countenance: the glorious fruit of thy womb.

Glory be to the Father, etc.

PSALM 129

Out of the depths I have cried to thee, O Lady: Lady, hear my prayer.

Let thine ears be attentive: to the voice of praise and of thy glorification.

Deliver me from the hand of my adversaries: confound their plans and their attempts against me.

Deliver me in the evil day: and in the day of death forget not my soul.

Lead me unto the harbor of salvation: may my name be written among the just.

Glory be to the Father, etc.

PSALM 130

Lady, my heart hath not been exalted: nor have mine eyes been lifted up.

The Lord hath blessed thee in His power: who by thee hath reduced to naught our enemies.

Blessed be He who hath sanctified thee: and who hath brought thee forth pure from thy mother's womb.

Blessed be He who hath overshadowed thee: and by His grace hath given thee fecundity.

Bless us, O Lady, and strengthen us in thy grace: that by thee we may be presented before the sight of the Lord.

Glory be to the Father, etc.

PSALM 131

Be mindful, O Lady, of David: and of all who invoke thy name.

Give us confidence in thy name: and let our adversaries be confounded.

Console us in the land of our pilgrimage: and relieve our poverty.

Give us, O holy Virgin, the bread of tears: and sorrow for our sins in the land of our sojourning.

Make the Blessed Fruit of thy womb propitious to us: that we may be filled with the grace of the Holy Spirit.

Glory be to the Father, etc.

PSALM 132

Behold how good and how pleasant, O Mary, it is: to love thy name.

Thy name is as oil poured out, and as an aromatic fragrance: to those who love it.

How great is the multitude of thy sweetness, O Lady: which thou hast prepared for those who love and hope in thee.

Be a refuge to the poor in tribulation: because thou art a staff to the poor and wretched.

Let them, I beseech thee, find grace with God: who invoke thy help in their needs.

Glory be to the Father, etc.

PSALM 133

Behold now, bless ye the Lady: all ye who hope in her holy name.

Rejoice with a great joy, you who exalt and glorify her: because you will be rejoiced by the plentifulness of her consolations.

Behold now with an overflowing bounty she will come down upon you: to console and to make glad your hearts.

Bless her, all her servants: and let her memory be the desire of your soul.

Bless her, all ye angels and saints of God: praise her wonders forever.

Glory be to the Father, etc.

PSALM 134

Praise the name of the Lord: bless the name of Mary, His Mother.

Be diligent in prayer to Mary: and she will raise up for you eternal delights.

Let us come to her in a contrite soul: and sinful cupidity will not besiege us.

He who thinks of her in tranquility of mind: shall find sweetness and the rest of peace.

Let us breathe forth our souls to her in our end: and she will lay open to us the courts of them that triumph.

Glory be to the Father, etc.

PSALM 135

Give praise to the Lord, for He is good: because by His most sweet Mother, the Virgin Mary, mercy is given to us.

Obtain for us, O Lady, the friendship of Jesus Christ: and keep us lest we should lose our innocence.

Repress our enemy by thy command: lest he should destroy in us the virtue of charity.

Illumine our ways and our paths: that we may know what is pleasing to God

Preserve in us what is naturally good: and may good graces be multiplied in us.

Glory be to the Father, etc.

PSALM 136

On the rivers of Babylon the Hebrews wept: but let us weep over our sins.

Let us cry out humbly to the Virgin and Mother: let us offer her our plaints and our sighs.

There is no propitiation to be found without her: nor salvation apart from her fruit.

By her, sins are purged away: and by her fruit, souls are made white.

By her is made satisfaction for sins; by her fruit health is bestowed.

Glory be to the Father, etc.

PSALM 137

will praise thee, O Lady, with my whole heart: because by thee I have ex-
erienced the clemency of Jesus Christ.

ear, O Lady, my words and prayers: and in the sight of angels I will sing
raise to thee.

n whatever day thou shalt invoke me, hear me: and multiply thy power in
y soul.

et all tribes and tongues praise thee: because by thee salvation is restored
o us.

rom all trouble save thy servants: and make them live under thy protection
nd peace.

lory be to the Father, etc.

PSALM 138

O Lady, thou hast tried me and known me: my ruin and my transgression.

hy mercy is plentiful above me: and thy clemency is great to me.

hine eye hath beheld mine imperfect being: and thine eyebrows have
nown my ways.

Ve have from the Holy Spirit an abundance of holy desires: and the stain of
in does not trouble our conscience.

he light of thy mercy makes serene our heart: and the sweetness of thy
eace recreates us.

lory be to the Father, etc.

PSALM 139

Deliver me, O Lady, from all evil: and from the infernal enemy defend me.

Against me he hath drawn his bow: and in his craftiness he hath laid snares for me.

Restrain his evil power: and powerfully crush his craft.

Turn back his iniquity on his own head: and let him speedily fall into the pit which he hath made.

But we will rejoice in thy service: and we will glory in thy praise.

Glory be to the Father, etc.

PSALM 140

O Lady, I have cried to thee, hear me: incline unto my prayer and to my supplication.

Let my supplication be directed as incense before thy face: both in the time of the evening sacrifice and in the morning.

Let not my heart turn aside into spiteful words: and let not the thought of wickedness upset my mind.

Make me submissive to the good pleasure of thy heart: and let me be conformed to thy actions.

With the sword of understanding pierce my heart: and with the dart of charity inflame my mind.

Glory be to the Father, etc.

PSALM 141

With my voice I have cried to Our Lady: I have humbly entreated her.

I have poured out my tears in her sight: and I have set before her my grief.

The enemy lieth in wait for my heel: he has spread his net before me.

Help me, O Lady, lest I fall before him: let-him be crushed beneath my feet.

Lead my soul out of prison: that it may praise thee and sing to the mighty God forever.

Glory be to the Father, etc.

PSALM 142

O Lady, hear my prayer: incline thine ear to my supplication.

The spiteful enemy hath persecuted my life: he hath cast on to the ground my ways.

He hath blackened me with his darkness: and my spirit is exceedingly troubled.

Turn not thy face away from me: that I may not fall together with them that tumble into the abyss.

Send forth thy light and thy grace: and repair anew my life and my conscience.

Glory be to the Father, etc.

PSALM 143

Blessed be thou, O Lady, who teaches thy servants to fight: and strengthens them against the enemy.

With thy lightnings and thy brightness scatter him: send forth thy darts, that thou mayest confound him.

Glorify from on high thy hand: and let thy servants sing thy praise and thy glory.

Raise up from earthly things our affection: from these eternal delights refresh our interior.

Kindle in our hearts the longing for heavenly things: and deign to refresh us with the joys of Paradise.

Glory be to the Father, etc.

PSALM 144

I will exalt thee, O Mother of the Son of God: and every day I will sing thy praises.

Generations and peoples will praise thy works: and the islands shall expect thy mercy.

The angels will utter the abundance of thy sweetness: and the saints will pronounce thy sweetness.

Our eyes hope in thee, O Lady: send us food and delightful nourishment.

My tongue shall speak thy praise: and I will bless thee for ever and ever.

Glory be to the Father, etc.

PSALM 145

My soul, praise Our Lady: I will glorify her as long as I live.

Never cease from her praises: and think of her every moment.

When my spirit shall go forth, Lady, let it be commended to thee: and in the unknown land be thou its guide.

Let not past sins trouble it: nor let it be disturbed by the meeting with the malignant one.

Lead it to the harbor of salvation: there let it await securely the coming of the Redeemer.

Glory be to the Father, etc.

PSALM 146

Praise the Lady, for a psalm is good: let the praise of her be pleasant and beautiful.

For she heals the broken-hearted: and she refreshes them with the ointment of piety.

Great is her power: and her clemency has no end.

Sing to her in jubilation: and in her praise sing a psalm to her.

Those who hope in the Lord are a good pleasure to her: and those who hope in her mercy.

Glory be to the Father, etc.

PSALM 147

Praise, O Jerusalem, Our Lady: glorify her also, O Sion.

For she buildeth up thy walls: and blesseth thy sons.

Let her grace nourish thee: let her give peace to thy borders.

The Most High hath sent forth His Word: and His power hath overshadowed her.

Let us raise our hearts and hands up to her: that we may feel her influence.

Glory be to the Father, etc.

PSALM 148

Let us praise Our Lady in the heavens: glorify her in the highest.

Praise her, all ye men and beasts: birds of the air, and fishes of the sea.

Praise her, sun and moon: stars, and the orbs of the planets.

Praise her, Cherubim and Seraphim: thrones and dominations and powers.

Praise her, all ye legions of angels: praise her all order of heavenly dwellers

Glory be to the Father, etc.

PSALM 149

ing a new song to Our Lady: her praise in the congregation of the just.

et the heavens rejoice in her glory: the isles of the sea and the whole world.

ire and water praise her: cold and heat, splendor and light.

et her praises be in the mouth of the just: and her glory in the band of the iumphant.

ity of God, be joyful in her: and for thy dwellers sing her a constant song.

lory be to the Father, etc.

PSALM 150

raise Our Lady in her saints: praise her in her virtues and miracles.

raise her, ye bands of Apostles: praise her, ye choirs and patriarchs and rophets.

raise her, ye army of martyrs; praise her, ye bands of doctors and confessors.

raise her in the college of virgins and the chaste: praise her, ye orders of ionks and holy anchorites.

raise her, ye monasteries of all religious: praise her, all the souls of all eavenly dwellers. Let every spirit praise Our Lady!

lory be to the Father, etc.

CANTICLES IN HONOR OF MARY

A CANTICLE ON THE MODEL OF ISAIAS (12)

I will praise thee, O Lady, because by thee the Lord has been rendered favorable unto me: and has consoled me.

Behold, Lady, thou art my savior: I will deal confidently in thee, and will not be confounded.

For thou art my strength and my praise in the Lord: and thou hast become salvation unto me.

I will draw waters in joy from the rivulet: and I will always invoke thy name.

Make known among the peoples the virtues of Our Lady: for her name is exceedingly sublime.

Exalt her and praise her, all the human race: because the Lord my God has given to thee such a mediatrix.

Glory be to the Father, etc.

A CANTICLE LIKE THAT OF EZECHIAS (IS. 38)

I have said in the midst of my days: I will go to Mary, that she may reconcile me to Christ.

I have sought the residue of my years: in the bitterness of my soul.

My generation is taken away: because my father and mother and all have forsaken me: but Mary hath taken me up.

I hoped in her in the morning, in the evening, and at midday: as a lion she hath broken all the bones of my sins.

And thou, O Lady, hast delivered my soul, that it should not be lost: and my only one from the hand of the dog.

Glory be to the Father, etc.

A CANTICLE LIKE THAT OF ANNA

My heart has rejoiced in the Lord: and my heart has exalted in my Lady.

For He who is mighty has done great things to me: by Mary His Mother.

There is no one holy as is Our Lady: who alone hath surpassed all.

Let the old things depart from our mouth: and let us speak with new tongues.

Exalt and praise Mary, O Sion and Jerusalem: for she is great amongst the ladies of Israel.

She makes poor and she enriches: she humbles and she exalts.

She is higher than the heavens: she is wider than the earth: is this Lady of ours.

Glory be to the Father, etc.

A CANTICLE LIKE THAT OF MARY (EXOD. 15)

Let us sing to Our Lady, the glorious Virgin Mary: let us bless her in hymns and praises.

The name of Our Lady is omnipotent after that of God: she hath cast the chariot of Pharaoh and his army into the sea.

Thy right hand, O Lady, is magnified in strength: because in the multitude of thy mercies thou hast prostrated mine adversaries.

Thou hast delivered me, O Lady, from the mouth of the lion: and as the mother her new-born infant hast thou received me.

O my most dear Lady: like the hen, cover me with thy wonderful protection.

I am all thine: and all my things are thine, Virgin blessed above all.

I will place thee as a seal upon my heart: because thy love is strong as death.

Glory be to the Father, etc.

A CANTICLE LIKE HABACUC'S (3)

O Lady, I have heard thy hearing: and I was astonished: I have considered thy works, and I have feared.

Lady, thy work: in the midst of the years thou hast quickened it.

I will praise thee, O Lady: for thou hast hidden these things from the wise, and hast revealed them to little ones.

Thy glory hath covered the heavens: and the earth is full of thy mercy.

Thou hast gone forth, O Virgin, in the salvation of thy people: to their salvation with Christ.

O blessed one, in thy hands is laid up our salvation: be mindful, O loving one, of our poverty.

He whom thou wilt save, will be saved: and he from whom thou shalt turn away thy face, will go down to destruction.

Glory be to the Father, etc.

A CANTICLE LIKE THAT OF MOSES (DEUT. 32)

Hear, ye heavens, what I shall speak of Mary: let the earth hear the words of my mouth.

Magnify her together with me: and let us exalt her name forever and ever.

O wicked and perverse generation: acknowledge our Lady for thy salvatrix.

Is she not thy mother, who hath possessed thee: and generated thee in faith?

If thou leavest her, thou art not the friend of the supreme Caesar: for without her He will not save thee.

Would that thou couldst understand, and be wise: and provide for thy last end!

As an infant without a nurse cannot live: so thou canst not have salvation without Our Lady.

Let thy soul thirst for her, hold her, and do not let her go: until she has blessed thee.

Let thy mouth be filled with her praises: sing her magnificence the whole day long.

Glory be to the Father, etc.

A CANTICLE LIKE THAT OF THE THREE CHILDREN

Bless, all works, our glorious Lady: praise and super exalt her forever.

Bless our Lady, ye Angels: ye heavens, bless our Lady.

Let every creature bless our Lady: whom the King wishes thus to be blessed.

Blessed be thou, O daughter of the most High King: who by thy fragrance surpassest all lilies.

Blessed be thou, crown of all ladies: blessed be thou, glory of Jerusalem.

Thy odor is like a full field which the Lord hath blessed: which overflows on those who bless thee, watering their whole souls and minds.

Whosoever shall bless thee, O Blessed Virgin: let him be blessed forever.

He who shall curse thee, O most white rose: let him be accursed.

Let not the abundance of wine and oil: depart from the house of thy servants.

In thy name let every knee bow: in Heaven, on earth, and in hell.

Let us bless God, who hath created thee: blessed be both thy parents who have begotten thee.

Blessed be thou, O Lady, in Heaven and on earth: worthy of praise, and glorious and super exalted forever.

Glory be to the Father, etc.

A CANTICLE LIKE THAT OF ZACHARIAS (LUKE 1)

Blessed be thou, O Lady and Mother of my God of Israel: who by thee hath quickened and hath wrought the redemption of His people.

And hath raised up a horn of salvation of thy chastity: in the house of David His servant.

As he spoke by the mouth of Isaias: and others of his holy prophets.

Give us salvation from our enemies, O Virgin of virgins: from the hand of those who hate us, give us peace.

And do thy mercy for us and our relations: that thou mayest be mindful of the testament of the Almighty God.

Which he hath sworn to our fathers: to Abraham and his seed forever;
That thus, being delivered from the hand of our enemies: we may serve Him in peace.

In sanctity and justice before thee: all our days.

And thou, O Mary, shalt be called the Prophet of God: for thou hast known that He hath regarded the humility of His handmaid.

By whom He hath given the knowledge of salvation to His people: in the remission of their sins.

By the bowels of the multitude of thy mercies: visit us, O Morning Star, the Orient from on high.

Enlighten the darknesses of those who sit in the shadow of death, and deign to instill into them the light of thy most Beloved Son.

Have mercy, O Mother of Mercies, on us miserable sinners, who neglect to do penance for our past sins: and daily commit so much that deserves penance.

Glory be to the Father, etc.

HYMN AFTER THE MODEL OF THE "TE DEUM"

We praise thee, O Mother of God: we confess thee, Mary, ever Virgin.

Thou art the Spouse of the Eternal Father: the whole earth venerates thee.

Thee all angels and archangels, thrones and principalities serve.

Thee all powers and all virtues of Heaven: and all dominations obey.

Before thee all the angelic choirs: the Cherubim and Seraphim exulting stand.

With unceasing voice every angelic creature proclaims thee:

Holy, holy, holy: Mary, Mother of God and Virgin!

Full are the heavens and the earth: of the majesty and glory of the fruit of thy womb.

Thee the glorious choir of Apostles: praise as the Mother of their Creator.

Thee the white-robed multitude of blessed martyrs: glorify as the Mother of Christ.

Thee the glorious army of Confessors: style the Temple of the Trinity.

Thee the amiable choir of holy virgins: preaches as the example of virginity and humility.

Thee the whole heavenly court: honoureth as Queen.

The Church, invoking thee, calls thee throughout the whole world: Mother of the Divine Majesty.

Venerating thee as the true Mother of the heavenly King: holy, sweet, and loving.

Thou art the Lady of Angels: thou art the gate of Paradise.

Thou art the ladder of glory: and of the heavenly kingdom.

Thou art the bridal chamber: thou art the ark of piety and grace.

Thou art the vein of mercy: thou art the Spouse and the Mother of the Eternal King.

Thou art the temple of the treasury of the Holy Ghost: thou art the noble throne of the whole blessed Trinity.

Thou art the Mediatrix of God, and the lover of men: the heavenly Illumina-trix of mortal men.

Thou art the inspirer of the warriors, the advocate of the poor: the compassionate refuge of sinners.

Thou art the distributrix of gifts: the barrier against demons and the proud, and their fear.

Thou art the Lady of the world, the Queen of Heaven: after God our only hope.

Thou art the salvation of them that call upon thee: the harbor of the ship-wrecked, the solace of the wretched, the refuge of those who perish.

Thou art the Mother of all the blessed, full of joy after God: the comfort of all the dwellers in Heaven.

Thou art the promotrix of the just, the one who gathers together those who stray: the promise of the patriarchs.

Thou art the truth of the prophets, the herald and teacher of the Apostles: the Mistress of the Evangelists.

Thou art the strength of martyrs, the example of confessors: the honor and the festivity of virgins.

Thou hast received into thy womb the Son of God: to deliver exiled man.

By thee is driven out the ancient enemy: and the kingdoms of Heaven are pened to believers.

Thou sittest together with thy Son: at the right hand of the Father.

Do thou intercede for us, O Virgin Mary: with Him who we believe will come to judge us.

We beseech thee, therefore, help us, thy servants: who have been redeemed with the Precious Blood of Thy Son.

Save thy people, O Lady: that we may be partakers of the inheritance of Thy Son.

And rule us: and keep us forever.

Day by day, O loving one: we salute thee.

And we desire to praise thee forever: with both mind and voice.

Deign, O sweet Mary, now and forever: to keep us without sin.

Have mercy on us, O loving one: have mercy on us.

Let thy great mercy be upon us: because we trust in thee, O Virgin Mary.

In thee, O sweet Mary, we hope: do thou defend us forever.

Praise becometh thee; empire is thine: to thee be power and glory forever.

Amen.

A MARIAN CREED AFTER THE MANNER
OF THAT OF ST. ATHANASIUS

Whoever wishes to be saved, before all must hold a firm faith as to Mary.

Which unless anyone shall keep whole and inviolate: without doubt he shall perish forever.

For she alone, remaining a virgin, hath brought forth: she alone hath destroyed all heresies.

Let the Jew be confounded and ashamed: who says that Christ was born from the seed of Joseph.

Let the Manichean be confounded who says: that Christ has an unreal body.

Let all be ashamed who say: that He derives His Body from any other source than Mary.

For the very same Son, who is the only-begotten of the Father in the Godhead: is the true and only begotten Son of the Virgin Mary.

In Heaven without a mother: on earth without a father.

For as the rational soul and the flesh because of the union in man is truly born from man: so Christ, both God and Man, is truly begotten by Mary, the Virgin.

Clothing Himself with flesh from the flesh of the Virgin: because so it behooved the human race to be redeemed.

Who according to the Divinity is equal to the Father: but according to His Humanity is less than the Father.

Conceived of the Holy Ghost in the womb of the Virgin Mary, and announced by the Angel: but nevertheless the Holy Spirit is not His Father.

Begotten in the world of the Virgin Mary without pain of the flesh: because He was conceived without carnal delight.

Whom the Mother hath fed with her milk: her breast full of heaven.

Whom the Angels surrounded as attendants at birth: announcing great joy to the shepherds.

He it is who was adored by the Magi with gifts, who fled from Herod into Egypt, who was baptized by John in the Jordan: was betrayed, seized, scourged, crucified, dead, and buried.

Who rose again with glory: and ascended into Heaven.

Who sent the Holy Spirit upon His disciples: and upon His Mother.

Whom He in the end took up into Heaven: where she sitteth at the right hand of her Son, never ceasing to make intercession for us.

This is the faith of the Virgin Mary: which, unless anyone faithfully and firmly believes, he cannot be saved.

The End

Made in the USA
Middletown, DE
03 April 2023

28158259R00059